CONTENTS

INTRODUCTION 4

BREAKING THE SOUND BARRIER 6

Supersonic 8

GAGARIN FALLS TO EARTH 10

The Space Race 12

SPAM IN A CAN 14

Splashdown 16

THE FIRST SPACE WALK 18

Down the Hatch 20

MAN ON THE MOON 22

One Small Step 24

APOLLO 13 26

A Successful Failure 28

FIRE IN SPACE 30

Mishaps in Space 32

THE CHALLENGER DISASTER 34

Failure to Launch 36

SPACESHIPONE 38

Going Suborbital 40

SPACE TOURIST 42

Orbital Outpost 44

GLOSSARY AND FURTHER INFORMATION 46

INDEX 48

INTRODUCTION

Space isn't very far away, but it's a difficult place to get to. Our adventures into space are littered with tales of triumph and disaster. Here are stories of bravery and daring from astronauts and examples of good luck and bad luck at the cutting edge of exploration.

Bruce McCandless II operates the Manned Maneuvering Unit (MMU) for the first time during a 1984 space shuttle mission.

Apollo 17 blasts off into the night sky on its way to the moon in 1972. It was the final lunar landing mission of the Apollo program.

FIND OUT MORE

BREAKING THE SOUND BARRIER

"Ouch, my ribs!"

Captain Charles "Chuck" Yeager winced. A few days before, he had broken two ribs when he had been thrown to the ground from a horse. Now he was being thrown around in the cockpit of his Bell X-1 aircraft. Yeager had kept his injuries a secret —and for a good reason.

He would never have been allowed to fly if his bosses had known about his cracked ribs. But this flight was an important one. He was a test pilot in the X-1 program, and he was aiming to do something no pilot had done before—fly faster than sound and so break the sound barrier.

Yeager's talent as a pilot, his wide experience, and his calmness made him a perfect test pilot. In test flights, Yeager had accelerated his bullet-shaped craft closer and closer to Mach 1—the speed of sound. Control problems at speeds approaching Mach 1 were ironed out, and today, October 14, 1947, was crunch day.

Yeager had clambered into the X-1 from the bomb bay of a Boeing B-29 Superfortress that had carried it into the sky. His broken bones prevented him from sealing the cockpit hatch with his arms, so fellow pilot Jack Ridley had rigged up a piece of broomstick to help do the job. The B-29 sped to an altitude of 25,000 feet (7,600 meters) over Rogers Lake, California.

Once released from the bomber, Yeager fired up the X-1's four rocket motors and accelerated away. Now running on just two engines, he nudged the aircraft toward the sound barrier. As had happened on previous flights, the aircraft was badly buffeted by shock waves. Yeager ignored the pain. He only had a small amount of fuel left and no time to lose. He relit the two rocket motors and gritted his teeth. The Machmeter crept up: 0.98, 0.99. Suddenly, the reading leapt even higher. Just as suddenly, the buffeting stopped.

FIND OUT MORE

Supersonic

Back at base, Yeager discovered he had reached Mach 1.06—a speed of 700 miles (1,126 kilometers) per hour. Having broken the sound barrier, he had become the fastest human of all time.

Chuck Yeager named the X-1 Glamorous Glennis *after his wife.*

The X-1's cockpit and instrument panel

Weird Flyers

The Bell X-1 was the first in a series of experimental "X" planes built to overcome the problems of high-speed flight. Its success was an important step on the journey to space, eventually reached by the Americans in 1961. NASA is still developing X-planes.

A collection of NASA research X-planes. They are, clockwise from top left, an XF-92A, X-5, D-558-2, X-4, X-1A and D-558-1. In the center is an X-3 Stiletto.

The forward-swept wings of the Grumman X-29 made it impossible to fly without the aid of computers.

In 2004 an unmanned X-43 test plane, using a type of jet engine called a scramjet, reached Mach 9.68, 6,388 mph (10,280 km/h).

Future astronaut Neil Armstrong (top) at the controls of the rocket-powered X-15 (above). In 1967 it reached Mach 6.72. It is still the world's fastest manned aircraft.

WINGLESS WONDERS

Planes without wings fly because they have "lifting bodies" that keep them up in the air. They were developed to discover the best shape for space reentry vehicles, such as the space shuttle.

The Martin X-24B, which flew in the 1970s, was designed as a space reentry vehicle and was used to test unpowered, gliding landings.

Three NASA "lifting body" planes are, from left to right, the X-24A, the M2-F3, and the HL-10.

GAGARIN FALLS TO EARTH
"…must…stay…conscious…"

Soviet cosmonaut Yuri Gagarin tried desperately not to black out as his spacecraft, *Vostok 1*, hurtled into the atmosphere. It was April 12, 1961, and Gagarin was now the very first man in space.

Gagarin had reached orbit without any major problems. *Vostok 1* had lifted off at 9:07 a.m. with Gagarin strapped into his descent module— a metal sphere just 7.5 feet (2.3 meters) across. "Here we go!" he screamed as the motors fired into life under him.

The two-stage rocket had worked almost perfectly, and just 11 minutes later Gagarin was in space, traveling at 28,000 miles (45,000 kilometers) per hour. After a single orbit of Earth, *Vostok 1*'s retro-rockets had fired. Soon after, the cone-shaped instrument module containing the retro-rocket should have separated. But a cable had become stuck, and *Vostok 1* started to tumble.

The reentry module was designed to protect Gagarin from the immense heat caused by air friction, but only if the module was at the right orientation. Right now it was out of control.

FIND OUT MORE

The Space Race

Vostok 1 flipped and spun for several minutes until the problem cable finally burned away. Then Gagarin was subjected to immense g-forces. He nearly fell unconscious, but he ejected from the module and landed safely by parachute.

The Soviet Union had beaten the United States in this round of the space race. Within two days, Yuri Gagarin was the most famous man on the planet.

The first woman in space was Soviet cosmonaut Valentina Tereshkova (left). Like Gagarin, she traveled in a Vostok capsule (right). She stayed in orbit for three days.

The head of the Soviet space program was rocket engineer Sergey Korolyov. His death in 1966 was a great blow to the Soviets' race into space.

The Huntsville Times

Man Enters Space

'So Close, Yet So Far,' Sighs Cape

U.S. Had Hoped For Own Launch

Soviet Officer Orbits Globe In 5-Ton Ship

Maximum Height Reached Reported As 188 Miles

Praise Is Heaped On Major Gagarin

First Man To Enter Space Is 27, Married, Father Of Two

To Keep Up, U.S.A. Must Run Like Hell'

ПЕРВАЯ В МИРЕ
ЖЕНЩИНА-КОСМОНАВТ
ВАЛЕНТИНА
ТЕРЕШКОВА
1963
10к ПОЧТА СССР

THE SOVIET SATELLITE

The Soviet Union won the race to put a satellite into orbit. *Sputnik 1* was launched in October 1957. It was just 22.8 inches (58 centimeters) across, but it sent signals back to Earth for 21 days.

Sputnik 1 showed that orbital flight was possible.

In January 1958, the United States launched Explorer 1, its first space satellite.

A dog called Laika was the first living creature sent into space. She died there.

In 1961, Ham the chimpanzee was sent into space by the United States. He returned unscathed.

ANIMAL PIONEERS

In the early days of the space race, nobody knew what effects weightlessness and the high g-forces of liftoff and reentry would have on humans. So animals, including mice, dogs and monkeys, were sent into space to see how they fared. Most returned safely.

Less than a month after Gagarin, Alan Shepard (above) became the first American in space.

SPAM IN A CAN

"Things are beginning to stack up a little..."

It was a bit of an understatement from US astronaut Gordon Cooper. The automatic control system of his Mercury spacecraft, *Faith 7*, had failed, and poisonous carbon dioxide was building up inside his capsule. Worse still, he was 124 miles (200 kilometers) up in space. Down on Earth, experts at Mercury Control were working frantically on the problem, quizzing Cooper about his instrument readings and then barking instructions.

Project Mercury was the American response to the launch of the Soviet Sputnik satellite in 1957. The goal was to put a human in space. The Mercury craft was fully automatic, which led the famous test pilot Chuck Yeager to describe the astronauts as "spam in a can." But Cooper and his fellow astronauts demanded, and got, a backup manual control system, too.

Cooper's flight in May 1963 was the final Mercury mission. The launch went exactly as planned.

"Feels good, buddy … all systems go," he reported to Mercury Control as he rode smoothly into orbit. He marveled at electrical storms below and the myriad of stars above as he flew around the Earth.

"Everything looks beautiful," fellow astronaut Alan Shepard reassured him from the ground. Cooper carried out experiments, measured his temperature and blood pressure, and snapped pictures. He even slept for a few orbits. The trouble began on orbit 19. A warning light came on—he was slowing down.

Two orbits later, an electrical blowout killed his automatic control system. It was lucky Cooper had a manual override—he would need it to get home. But he would have to get his reentry perfect. The slightest mistake and *Faith 7* would bounce off the atmosphere, or incinerate as he traveled through it.

FIND OUT MORE

Splashdown

Using the grid lines he had drawn on the window, Cooper adjusted the angle of the spacecraft. On command from Mercury Control, he fired the retro-rockets. Minutes later *Faith 7*, flying with parachutes, splashed into the Pacific exactly on target.

An Atlas rocket with the Faith 7 *Mercury capsule waits for liftoff.*

Navy divers attend Gordon Cooper's capsule.

The Mercury Control center, Cape Canaveral, Florida

The seven Mercury astronauts were Gordon Cooper (far left), Wally Schirra (partially obscured), Alan Shepard, Gus Grissom, John Glenn, Donald "Deke" Slayton, and Scott Carpenter.

THE MAGNIFICENT SEVEN

Gordon Cooper was one of seven top-notch military pilots selected for Project Mercury. They were America's first astronauts, and they became heroes even before going into space. Six of them flew on Mercury missions.

A Snug Fit

The cone-shaped, one-man Mercury capsule was just 6.2 feet (1.9 meters) across. The control and navigation equipment left little space for the astronaut, who was strapped into a fitted seat to protect him from g-forces during launch and reentry.

Main parachute

Retro rocket and heat shield

John Glenn (right) was the first American to orbit the Earth.

John Glenn's Mercury capsule, called Friendship 7, blasts off atop an Atlas rocket (right). The rocket was an adapted Atlas intercontinental ballistic missile.

The Gemini project (above) followed the Mercury program.

THE FIRST SPACE WALK
"Belyayev! Help, I'm stuck."

Cosmonaut Pavel Belyayev was in the relative safety of the *Voskhod 2* spacecraft, but Alexei Leonov was still outside. His excitement at becoming the first man to "walk" in space evaporated. As hard as he tried, he couldn't squeeze back into the spacecraft's airlock.

It was March 18, 1965, and *Voskhod 2* was in orbit above the Earth. Ten minutes earlier Leonov had climbed into Volga, the exterior airlock that inflated in orbit. With the inner hatch closed, the air was pumped out. Then Leonov had opened the outer door and climbed out into space.

This was easy! He was protected from the vacuum of space by his pressurized spacesuit and attached to the spacecraft by a long umbilical cable. Leonov marveled at the view of Earth. "Pavel, I can see past the Straits of Gibraltar, all the way to the Caspian Sea!" he exclaimed. During the past 20 minutes he had "walked" from north-central Africa to eastern Siberia. Now it was time to return to the spacecraft.

It was then that Leonov noticed that his spacesuit had ballooned. It was now rigid, and he couldn't bend his legs! Half in and half out of the airlock, he was in desperate trouble. He realized his only chance was to depressurize the suit. There was a real danger of getting the "bends" (decompression sickness), but it was a risk he had to take. Leonov reached for the valve.

FIND OUT MORE

Down The Hatch

Leonov was lucky. With the suit deflated, he was able to haul himself into the airlock. He was exhausted, and it was still a struggle to turn and close the outer hatch. Later, with Volga jettisoned, *Voskhod 2* returned safely to Earth.

Alexei Leonov took these self-portraits on the first-ever space walk in 1965.

Edward White performs the first US space walk during the Gemini 4 mission of 1965.

The Voskhod air lock and Berkut space suit

EXTRAVEHICULAR ACTIVITY

The fancy name for a space walk, extravehicular activity (EVA for short) means leaving a spacecraft and going out into space. It's risky but necessary to check the spacecraft for damage and to repair and maintain satellites in orbit.

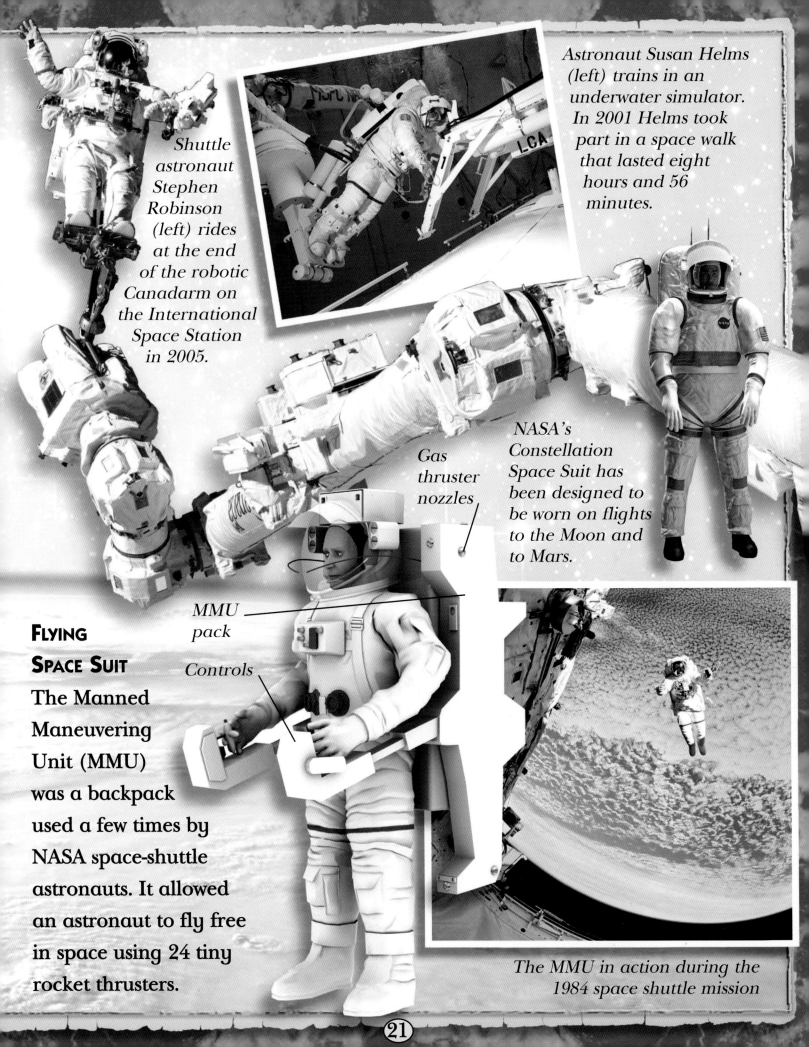

Shuttle astronaut Stephen Robinson (left) rides at the end of the robotic Canadarm on the International Space Station in 2005.

Astronaut Susan Helms (left) trains in an underwater simulator. In 2001 Helms took part in a space walk that lasted eight hours and 56 minutes.

Gas thruster nozzles

NASA's Constellation Space Suit has been designed to be worn on flights to the Moon and to Mars.

MMU pack

Controls

FLYING SPACE SUIT

The Manned Maneuvering Unit (MMU) was a backpack used a few times by NASA space-shuttle astronauts. It allowed an astronaut to fly free in space using 24 tiny rocket thrusters.

The MMU in action during the 1984 space shuttle mission

MAN ON THE MOON

"Okay *Eagle*, one minute, you guys take care."

Mike Collins wished his fellow *Apollo 11* astronauts farewell. Through the window of Apollo's command module, *Columbia*, he had checked that the landing legs of the lunar module, *Eagle*, were down and locked. Neil Armstrong and Buzz Aldrin were about to descend to the surface of the moon.

It was July 20, 1969. *Apollo 11* had left Earth four days earlier, launched by a Saturn V rocket from Cape Kennedy. Once in orbit of the moon, *Columbia* separated itself from *Saturn* and connected with *Eagle*. The mission was the culmination of a program that had begun in 1961 when President John F. Kennedy had committed the United States to landing a man on the moon. Years of research, dozens of test flights, and billions of dollars later, success was resting on the weightless shoulders of Armstrong and Aldrin.

One of Armstrong's footprints

Eagle was heading for the Sea of Tranquillity—a flat region with few large craters. The descent engine fired briefly and down they went. All went smoothly until *Eagle* was about 5,900 feet (1,800 meters) above the surface. Then Armstrong reported a warning light in the lunar module. Perhaps they were descending too fast? Experts at Mission Control in Houston reassured them that it was nothing to worry about —just a computer overload. The warning light came on again at 2,950 feet (900 meters) above the surface. Again they ignored it. Up ahead Armstrong could see the spot where they would touch down—it was a boulder-filled crater! He quickly took manual control. Then came a warning from Mission Control: "Neil, be advised, you have 30 seconds of fuel left." Back on Earth, they waited with bated breath.

FIND OUT MORE

One Small Step

"**C**ontact light!" said Aldrin's calm voice. Then came Armstrong's words: "Houston, Tranquillity Base here. The *Eagle* has landed!" They had just 20 seconds of fuel left. Six hours later, Armstrong climbed down the ladder and onto the lunar surface.

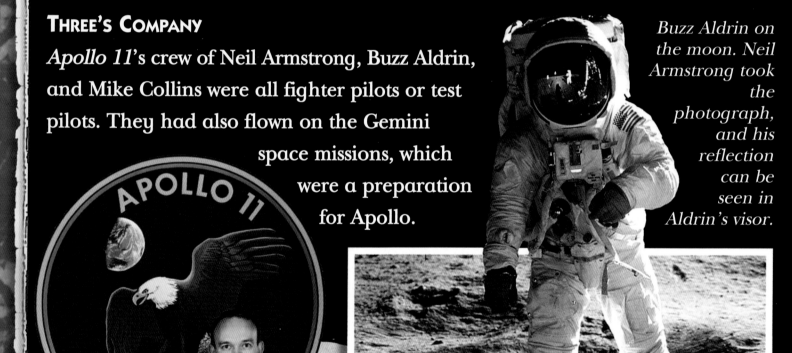

"That's one small step for man, one giant leap for mankind," said Armstrong as he stepped onto the moon.

THREE'S COMPANY

Apollo 11's crew of Neil Armstrong, Buzz Aldrin, and Mike Collins were all fighter pilots or test pilots. They had also flown on the Gemini space missions, which were a preparation for Apollo.

Buzz Aldrin on the moon. Neil Armstrong took the photograph, and his reflection can be seen in Aldrin's visor.

The Apollo 11 crew were (from left) Armstrong, Collins, and Aldrin.

LAST MEN ON THE MOON

Six more Apollo missions followed in the three years after *Apollo 11*. *Apollo 13* did not land (see page 26), but 12 more astronauts walked on the moon, surveying and carrying out experiments. The final mission was *Apollo 17*.

In 1959 the Soviet Union's Luna 2 *(left)* became the first spacecraft to land on the moon. In 1970 they landed Lunokhod 1 *(below)*, a moon vehicle.

The three-stage Saturn V rocket stood 364 feet (111 meters) tall and weighed 3,000 tons (2,700 metric tons). The spacecraft weighed 50 tons (45 metric tons).

Aldrin removes scientific equipment from the Lunar Module Eagle.

Each Apollo mission brought moon samples of rock and dust back from the moon. They were billions of years old.

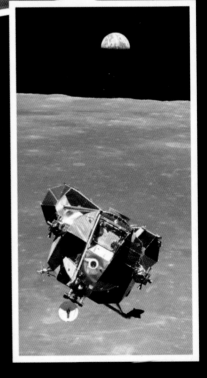

After over 21 hours on the moon's surface, the Eagle returns to the command module.

A lunar rover traveled with Apollo 15, 16, and 17. It allowed the astronauts to explore many miles away from the lunar module.

APOLLO 13

"That's it Fred—we've lost the moon."

Jim Lovell realized that his hopes of landing on the moon during this third manned mission were gone. The Fred he spoke to was Fred Haise, the astronaut who should have accompanied Lovell to the lunar surface. But 205,000 miles (330,000 kilometers) from Earth, and with their spacecraft badly damaged, the chances of reaching the lunar surface now were nil. The chances of getting home alive weren't much better.

Together with John "Jack" Swigert, Commander Lovell and Fred Haise were aboard *Apollo 13*. They had left Earth on April 11, 1970. Halfway to the moon, during the third day of the flight, Swigert had flicked a switch to stir the oxygen tanks. Moments later the crew heard a muffled bang, and the whole spacecraft shook.

"Houston, we've had a problem." Swigert announced on the intercom, as he stared at the warning light.

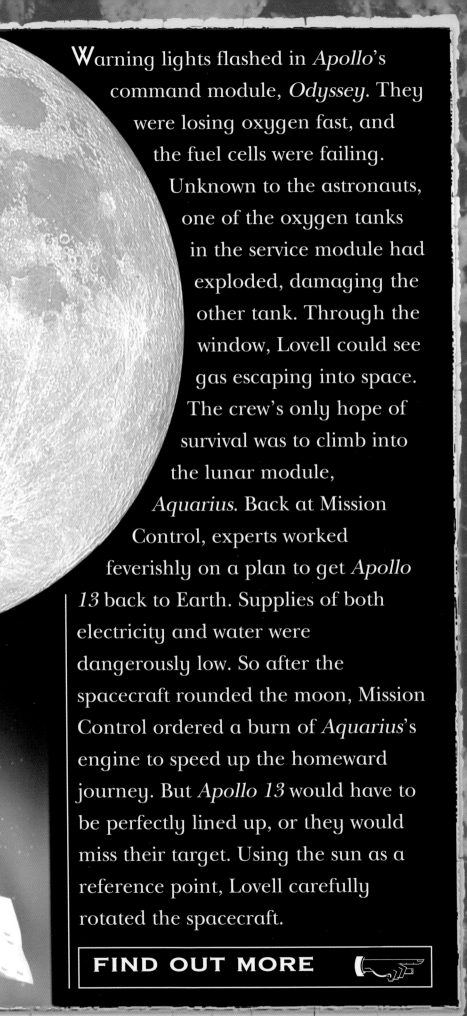

Warning lights flashed in *Apollo*'s command module, *Odyssey*. They were losing oxygen fast, and the fuel cells were failing. Unknown to the astronauts, one of the oxygen tanks in the service module had exploded, damaging the other tank. Through the window, Lovell could see gas escaping into space. The crew's only hope of survival was to climb into the lunar module, *Aquarius*. Back at Mission Control, experts worked feverishly on a plan to get *Apollo 13* back to Earth. Supplies of both electricity and water were dangerously low. So after the spacecraft rounded the moon, Mission Control ordered a burn of *Aquarius*'s engine to speed up the homeward journey. But *Apollo 13* would have to be perfectly lined up, or they would miss their target. Using the sun as a reference point, Lovell carefully rotated the spacecraft.

FIND OUT MORE

A Successful Failure

"**W**e've got it!" cried Lovell, as the sun lined up perfectly. With only essential equipment switched on to conserve electricity, the crew settled down for a cold trip home. Soon another problem raised its head.

Mission Control moments before the accident

On Earth, Mission Control worked to make an air filter.

DO IT YOURSELF

A warning light indicated a buildup of carbon dioxide gas. The air filters needed replacing, but the spares did not fit. With help from engineers on the ground, the crew solved the problem.

The damaged service module

The crew used spare plastic tubes, cardboard, and sticky tape to rig up air filters.

THE LUNAR LIFEBOAT

Apollo 13's lunar module, *Aquarius*, was a separate spacecraft from the command and service modules. With its own oxygen tanks and electrical batteries, it could support the astronauts on their journey home.

Service module   Command module

Lunar module engine

Lunar module

A few hours from home, the crew climbed back into the command module and jettisoned Aquarius (below). The lunar module fell to Earth.

A tense moment in Mission Control

On April 17, the command module splash landed safely (left).

Members of Mission Control (above) cheer as Lovell, Swigert, and Haise land back on Earth and are taken aboard the USS Iwo Jima (right).

FIRE IN SPACE
"Be prepared for decompression!"

American astronaut Jerry Linenger screamed a warning to his fellow crew members on the Mir space station. As astronauts, their worst nightmare had become a reality —fire was raging on board. It was threatening to burn a hole in the spacecraft's skin. If it did, they would lose all of their air. They had to put out the flames—or perish in space.

On February 24, 1997, a new crew had arrived in a Soyuz spacecraft, so there were now six men on Mir. It was cramped, and oxygen supplies were limited. After dinner, Linenger had made his way to check some experiments in the Specktr module, while Russian cosmonaut Alexander Lazutkin had gone to the Kvant module to activate a fresh oxygen canister. Suddenly an alarm siren began to wail. At first Linenger was not too concerned—alarms were going off all the time on Mir. He went to check it out anyway. As he arrived in the core module, Linenger bumped into Vasily Tsibliev.

"Very serious. Fire!" Tsibliev had shouted. Linenger looked into the Kvant module and was horrified to see a three-foot (1-meter) long flame shooting out of an oxygen canister. Choking on acrid smoke, the crew struggled to strap on respirators. Then both Linenger and cosmonaut Valeri Korzun grabbed fire extinguishers. Korzun sprayed his, but the fire kept raging.

FIND OUT MORE

Mishaps in Space

Linenger aimed his extinguisher at the module wall to keep the wall cool. After burning for 14 minutes, the fire went out. The smoke slowly cleared. There was some damage, but the crew members were fine except for a few minor burns.

Jerry Linenger wears an oxygen mask after the fire.

SKYLAB TROUBLES

Skylab was an American space station launched in 1973. It was made from part of a Saturn V rocket. But it was damaged during the launch, losing one of its solar arrays. Astronauts managed to fix the problem during a space walk.

Despite damage at the launch in 1973, Skylab (right) stayed in space until 1979.

MORE MIR PROBLEMS

Just months after the 1997 fire, a supply craft crashed into Mir during docking, damaging the Specktr module and a solar panel. The module had to be sealed off because of an air leak.

The Mir space station was launched in 1983. It was almost worn out by the time it was abandoned in 1998.

The damage to Mir's solar array (above left) was caused by a collision with an out-of-control Progress supply craft (above).

Donald Slayton (left) and Alexei Leonov pictured in 1975 during the American Apollo and Soviet Soyuz joint space mission (above). On reentry, the Apollo capsule filled with fumes, nearly suffocating the crew.

THE *CHALLENGER* DISASTER
"Roger, go at throttle up."

Dick Scobee, commander of the space shuttle *Challenger*, confirmed that he had heard a message from Mission Control— engine power had been increased. Scobee was one of seven astronauts on board the rumbling spacecraft. Other crew members were engineers, scientists, and a schoolteacher. In the cargo bay under them was a communications satellite, ready to be launched into orbit.

The space shuttle is a reusable spacecraft designed to ferry people and equipment into Earth's orbit. It reaches space like a rocket, but returns to the ground like a plane. The shuttle was intended to make space flight cheaper: other "launch vehicles" can only be used once. It is possibly the most complex flying machine ever built.

The plane-like part of a shuttle is called the orbiter. Inside are the crew cabin and the cargo bay. The main engines and maneuvering engines sit at the rear. As for all shuttle launches, *Challenger* had been bolted to a giant external fuel tank (containing fuel for its engines) and two solid rocket boosters to give it an extra push to get off the launch pad.

Challenger was the workhorse of NASA's shuttle fleet. This flight, on January 28, 1986, was already its tenth. The shuttle program had been a great success. The four space shuttles had hauled a wide range of payloads into orbit, including civilian and military satellites and the science laboratory Spacelab. Their crews had repaired several satellites in space, often during space walks. So far there had been no accidents, and launches had now become routine.

Challenger was only into its second minute of flight, but it had already reached 20,000 feet (6 kilometers) above the Earth's surface and was traveling at 1,000 miles (1,600 kilometers) per hour. The crew must have felt a push on their backs during the "throttle up."

The huge crowd watching from below could see the shuttle's vapor trail curving into the blue sky. Suddenly, a plume of smoke appeared at its tip. Turning to the person next to her, one observer asked, "This is my first time watching a shuttle launch—is that normal?"

FIND OUT MORE

The crew of the Challenger. In the back row from left to right: Ellison S. Onizuka, Christa McAuliffe, Greg Jarvis, and Judy Resnik. In the front row from left to right: Michael J. Smith, Dick Scobee, and Ron McNair.

Failure to Launch

Due to a faulty solid rocket booster, *Challenger* had disintegrated in midair, killing its crew. The accident was a huge setback that grounded the shuttle program for over two years.

A solid rocket booster flies free as pieces of glowing wreckage shoot through the air moments after the failure of Challenger.

Just before the explosion, a burst of flame was seen coming from Challenger's right rocket booster.

When Challenger exploded, there was confusion and disbelief at Mission Control. They lost all contact with the crew.

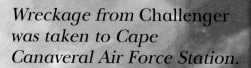

Wreckage from Challenger was taken to Cape Canaveral Air Force Station.

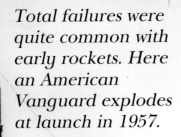

Total failures were quite common with early rockets. Here an American Vanguard explodes at launch in 1957.

APOLLO 1 FIRE

In 1967 three *Apollo 1* astronauts were killed by a fire in their capsule. The fire broke out during a training exercise on the ground a month before they were due to go into space.

The burnt-out command module of Apollo 1

Apollo 1's crew

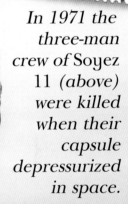

In 1971 the three-man crew of Soyez 11 (above) were killed when their capsule depressurized in space.

In 1996, a Chinese Long March 3B rocket veered off course. It hit a local village, killing dozens of people.

THE COLUMBIA DISASTER

On February 1, 2003, the shuttle *Columbia* broke apart during re-entry. The crew of seven were killed. One of its heat-resistant tiles had been knocked off during launch. It was two years before another shuttle flew.

A video still shows Columbia's flight deck before the disaster (above left). A photo shows wreckage gathered for investigation (above).

SPACESHIPONE
"Now this is FUN!"

Mike Melvill was enjoying himself. He was 328,000 feet (100 kilometers) above the Earth in *SpaceShipOne* (SS1). As the spacecraft stopped gaining altitude and began to fall back toward the Earth, he was weightless in his pilot's seat. It was September 29, 2004, and Melvill was on flight number 16P, the first qualifying flight in the Tier One program run by the Scaled Composites company. The program was designed to win a very special prize—the Ansari X Prize—for the first nongovernmental organization to get a reusable manned craft into space. The flight had started when *SpaceShipOne* was dropped by its White Knight carrier plane at an altitude of 50,000 feet (15 kilometers).

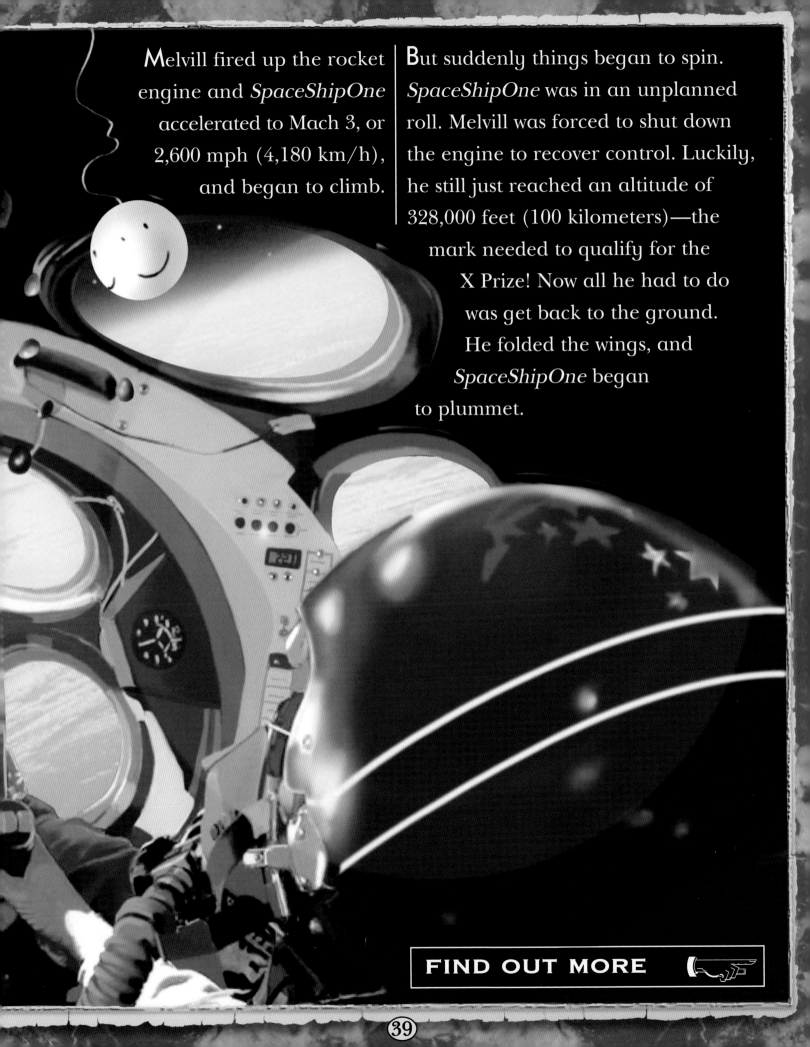

Melvill fired up the rocket engine and *SpaceShipOne* accelerated to Mach 3, or 2,600 mph (4,180 km/h), and began to climb.

But suddenly things began to spin. *SpaceShipOne* was in an unplanned roll. Melvill was forced to shut down the engine to recover control. Luckily, he still just reached an altitude of 328,000 feet (100 kilometers)—the mark needed to qualify for the X Prize! Now all he had to do was get back to the ground. He folded the wings, and *SpaceShipOne* began to plummet.

FIND OUT MORE

Going Suborbital

The wings kept *SpaceShipOne* at the right angle as it plunged into the atmosphere. Just 25 minutes after take-off Melvill glided smoothly onto the runway. Success! A few days later, *SpaceShipOne* claimed the $10 million prize by repeating the flight.

Mike Melvill waves in triumph after landing SpaceShipOne.

SpaceShipOne was carried into the air by a custom-built White Knight jet aircraft.

THE X PRIZE

The Ansari X Prize was set up to encourage private manned space flight and to boost the idea of space tourism. To win, a spacecraft capable of carrying three people had to reach an altitude of 328,000 feet (100 kilometers) and then repeat the feat within two weeks.

Armadillo Aerospace's Pixel rocket undergoes a flight test. The Pixel rocket was a rival to SpaceShipOne for the Ansari X prize.

SpaceShipOne now hangs in the National Air and Space Museum in Washington, DC.

A WhiteKnightTwo jet (above) *will be used to launch SpaceShipTwo.*

THE FUTURE IS HERE

The Scaled Composites company has teamed up with Virgin to build *SpaceShipTwo* (SS2), designed to carry two pilots and six tourists into space and then stay there for a few minutes before returning to the ground. It will be launched by a WhiteKnightTwo jet aircraft.

Other companies plan to send tourists into space. Right is a mock-up of the interior of the EADS Astrium Space Tourism vehicle.

The interior of SpaceShipTwo (above)

SpaceShipTwo *is based on SpaceShipOne, but it is larger (above). It uses the same folding wing system to remain stable during its descent back into the atmosphere.*

SPACE TOURIST

"Soyuz TMA-9, your approach is looking good."

The Soyuz spacecraft crept toward the International Space Station (ISS). Aboard was 40-year-old Anousheh Ansari, an Iranian-American businesswoman and only the world's fourth space tourist. It was September 20, 2006, and despite sickness and headaches brought on by weightlessness, Ansari was happy and excited to finally arrive at the ISS.

Over the next few days, Ansari settled into space-station routine. Between carrying out experiments, taking photographs, sharing meals, and chatting with her fellow astronauts, she spent hours literally watching the world go by 218 miles (350 kilometers) below. She was mesmerized by complex cloud formations by day and electrical storms by night. She also found time to write a blog so that people back on Earth could follow her experiences in space.

"I am having a wonderful time here. It's been more than what I expected, and I am enjoying every single second of it," she wrote.

After nine days aboard the ISS, it was time to return home to Earth. As the *Soyuz TMA-8* spacecraft began to dip into the atmosphere, flight engineer Jeffrey Williams told Ansari to get ready for a "roller coaster ride."

FIND OUT MORE

Orbital Outpost

"**I**t was like having an elephant on my chest," said Ansari of the g-forces during reentry. "I hope that my trip becomes an inspiration for all of you to follow your dreams," she told audiences during her worldwide lecture tour.

Anousheh Ansari makes a live television broadcast with the rest of the crew of the ISS. Six space tourists have now visited the station.

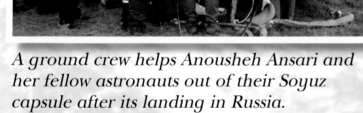

A ground crew helps Anousheh Ansari and her fellow astronauts out of their Soyuz capsule after its landing in Russia.

AN INTERNATIONAL SUCCESS STORY

The International Space Station is a joint venture between the United States, Russia, Europe, and Japan. Its first module was put into orbit in 1998, and it was completed in May

The Destiny Laboratory was supplied by the United States in 2001.

2011. The station is a research laboratory in space, where scientists study the effects on people of living in space and carry out experiments in zero gravity. The station is made up of habitation, science, and service modules, supplied and operated by the different countries.

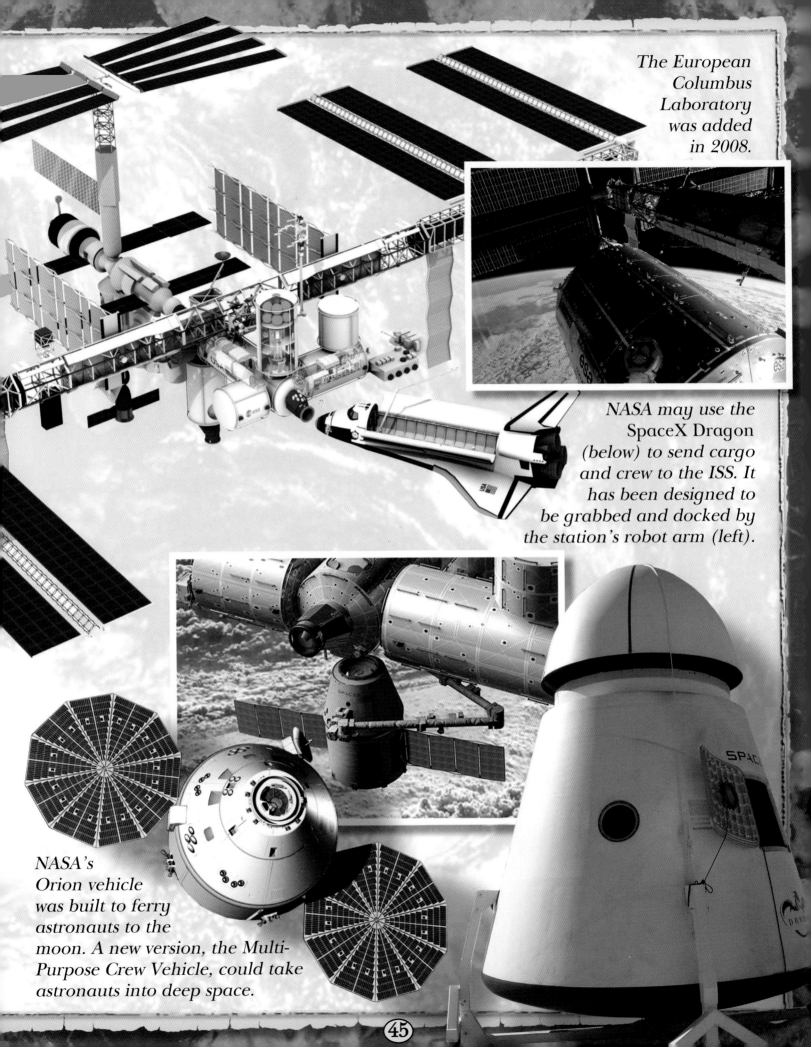

The European Columbus Laboratory was added in 2008.

NASA may use the SpaceX Dragon (below) to send cargo and crew to the ISS. It has been designed to be grabbed and docked by the station's robot arm (left).

NASA's Orion vehicle was built to ferry astronauts to the moon. A new version, the Multi-Purpose Crew Vehicle, could take astronauts into deep space.

GLOSSARY

Airlock A chamber between the inside of a spacecraft and space, with a door at each end to allow astronauts to go out into space.

Buffeted Hit or pushed with force.

Cosmonaut The Russian word for astronaut.

g-force A force on an astronaut's body caused by going faster or slower.

Intercontinental ballistic missile A military missile designed to carry a bomb thousands of miles.

Jettisoned Thrown or dropped off the main part of a ship or shuttle.

Mach The ratio of the speed of a body to the speed of sound in an area.

Navigation The science of plotting a route and directing an aircraft, spacecraft, or vehicle along it.

Reentry vehicle A spacecraft that returns to the Earth (reentering the atmosphere to do so).

Respirator A portable oxygen supply and face mask.

Retro-rocket A rocket engine that is fired to slow down a spacecraft.

Sound barrier An aerodynamic barrier that aircraft have to break through to go faster than the speed of sound.

Umbilical cable A cable carrying oxygen and communications to an astronaut on a space walk.

Weightlessness A state in which an object or body does not seem to have any apparent weight.

Zero gravity A state of weightlessness.

FURTHER INFORMATION

ORGANIZATIONS AND WEB SITES

Chuck Yeager
PO Box 579
Penn Valley, CA 95946
Web site:
http://www.chuckyeager.com

Kennedy Space Center
State Road 405
Titusville, FL 32899
(321) 449-4444
Web site:
http://www.kennedyspacecenter.com

National Aeronautics and Space
Administration (NASA)
Suite 5K39
Washington, DC 20546-0001
(202) 358-0001
Web site: http://www.nasa.gov

Smithsonian National Air and Space
Museum
Independence Ave at 6th Street, SW
Washington, DC 20560
(202) 633-2214
Web site: http://www.nasm.si.edu

FOR FURTHER READING

Glover, Linda K. *National Geographic Encyclopedia of Space*. Washington, D.C.: National Geographic Society, 2005.

Hibbert, Claire. *The Inside & Out Guide to Spacecraft*. Chicago, IL: Heinemann Library, 2006.

Jeffrey, Gary and Mike Lacey. *Graphic Discoveries: Incredible Space Missions*. New York, NY: Rosen Publishing, 2007.

Nipaul, Devi. *The International Space Station: An Orbiting Laboratory*. Danbury, CT: Children's Press, September 2004.

West, David and Jim Robins. *Graphic Careers: Astronauts*. New York, NY: Rosen Publishing, 2008.

INDEX

A
Aldrin, Buzz, 23–25
Ansari, Anousheh, 42–44
Apollo 1, 37
Apollo 11, 23–25
Apollo 13, 25–29
Apollo 15, 25
Apollo 16, 25
Apollo 17, 5, 25
Aquarius, 27, 29
Armstrong, Neil, 9, 23–24

B
Bell X-1, 6–8
Belyayev, Pavel, 18–19

C
Challenger, 34–36
Collins, Mike, 23–24
Columbia, 37
Cooper, Gordon, 14–16

E
Eagle, 22–25
EVA, 20
Explorer 1, 13

F
Faith 7, 14–16
Friendship 7, 17

G
Gagarin, Yuri, 10–13

Gemini 4, 20
Gemini missions, 24
Gemini project, 17
Glenn, John, 16–17

H
Haise, Fred, 26, 29

I
International Space
    Station, 21, 42–44

K
Korolyov, Sergey, 12

L
Lazutkin, Alexander, 31
Leonov, Alexei, 18–20, 33
Linenger, Jerry, 30–32
Lovell, Jim, 26–29
Luna 2, 25

M
McCandless, Bruce II, 4
Melvill, Mike, 38–40
Mir, 30–31, 33
MMU, 4, 21

N
NASA, 8–9, 21, 35, 45

P
Project Mercury, 14–17

R
Resnik, Judy, 36

S
Saturn V, 23, 25, 32
Scobee, Dick, 34, 36
Shepard, Alan, 13, 15–16
Skylab, 32
sound barrier, 6–7, 8
Soyuz 11, 37
Soyuz TMA-8, 43
Soyuz TMA-9, 42
SpaceShipOne, 38–41
SpaceShipTwo, 41
SpaceX Dragon, 45
Sputnik 1, 13, 15
Swigert, John, 26, 29

T
Tereshkova, Valentina,
    12
Tsibliev, Vasily, 31

V
Voskhod 2, 18, 20
Vostok 1, 10–11

X
X-1 program, 6–8
X-planes, 8–9

Y
Yeager, Chuck, 6–8, 15

WEB SITES